D0757645

COMMUNITY · CONNECTIONS

?

HOW DO THEY HELP?
ROTARY CLUBS

BY KATIE MARSICO

CHERRY LAKE
Publishing

Published in the United States of America by Cherry Lake Publishing
Ann Arbor, Michigan
www.cherrylakepublishing.com

Content Adviser: Rob Fischer, Ph.D., Professor and Director, Master of Nonprofit
Organizations, Jack, Joseph, and Morton Mandel School of Applied Social Sciences,
Case Western Reserve University
Reading Adviser: Marla Conn MS, Ed., Literacy specialist, Read-Ability, Inc.

Photo Credits: © Dan Kitwood/Thinkstock, cover, 1, 17; © Paula Bronstein/Thinkstock, 5;
© Riccardo Mayer/Shutterstock, 7; © Joseph Sohm/Shutterstock, 9; © CORBIS, 11; © Koco77
I Dreamstime.com - Hunger Run (Rome) - World Food Programme - Rotary Photo, 13; © age
fotostock / Alamy Stock Photo, 15; © Jmrobledo I Dreamstime.com - Computer Room Donated
By Rotary International Photo, 19; © OlegD/Shutterstock, 21

LIBRARY OF CONGRESS CATALOGING-IN-PUBLICATION DATA
Names: Marsico, Katie, 1980- author.
Title: Rotary clubs / by Katie Marsico.
Description: Ann Arbor, Michigan : Cherry Lake Publishing, [2016] I
Series: Community connections: how do they help? I Includes bibliographical
   references and index.
Identifiers: LCCN 2015049388I ISBN 9781634710534 (hardcover) I
   ISBN 9781634711524 (pdf) I ISBN 9781634712514 (pbk.) I
   ISBN 9781634713504 (ebook)
Subjects: LCSH: Rotary International—Juvenile literature. I
   Businesspeople–Societies, etc.—Juvenile literature. I Voluntarism—Juvenile literature. I
   Civic improvement—Juvenile literature. I Community development—Juvenile literature.
Classification: LCC HF5001.R79 M37 2016 I DDC 369.5/2—dc23
LC record available at http://lccn.loc.gov/2015049388

Cherry Lake Publishing would like to acknowledge the
work of The Partnership for 21st Century Learning.
Please visit www.p21.org for more information.

Printed in the United States of America
Corporate Graphics
CLFA11

ROTARY CLUBS

CONTENTS

SERVICES THAT SAVE LIVES

In 1988, health officials reported around 350,000 cases of polio worldwide. This disease attacks a person's nervous system and causes paralysis, or an inability to move. Sometimes it even leads to death.

Thanks to Rotary clubs, far fewer people suffer from polio today. By providing **immunizations**,

Today, polio is uncommon in the United States but it is still a problem in some areas of the world.

Are you able to guess how many people Rotary clubs have helped immunize against polio? If you guessed more than 2 billion, you're right! As a result, in 2013, there were only 407 reported cases of the disease.

Rotary clubs have helped reduce occurrences of the illness by 99 percent!

Rotary clubs also promote peace and care for families. They support education, ensure that people have clean water, and help local **economies** grow as well.

Rotary clubs are **nonprofit** organizations made up of business and professional leaders. Members—called Rotarians—work together to create positive changes in their own communities and across the globe.

Ensuring that all communities have access to fresh water is an important goal of Rotary clubs.

Rotary clubs currently exist in more than 200 countries, including the United States and Canada. Does your community have one of these service organizations? Do you know any Rotarians? Ask your parents or look online for answers!

THE PAST AND PRESENT

Attorney Paul P. Harris developed the first Rotary club in Chicago, Illinois, in 1905. Harris wanted to give local businessmen an opportunity to gather, hold discussions, and build lasting friendships. Members used the name "Rotary" because they rotated, or took turns, hosting

The Rotary's slogan is "Service Above Self." This means members help others before helping themselves.

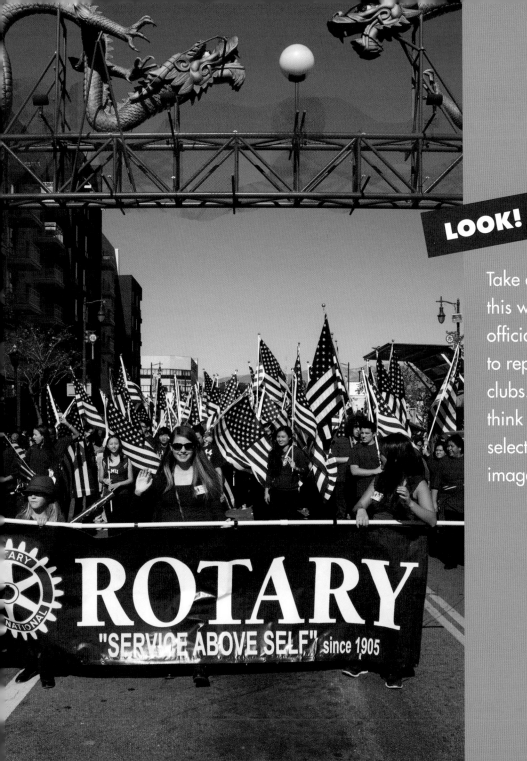

Take a close look at this wheel. It is the official symbol used to represent Rotary clubs. Why do you think Rotarians selected this particular image?

ROTARY

"SERVICE ABOVE SELF" since 1905

meetings in each of their offices. During the next few decades, professionals started forming similar organizations in other areas.

Eventually, Rotarians focused on setting high **ethical** standards in business in order to better serve their communities. They also joined forces with other volunteer groups and **humanitarian** organizations to fund service projects. During World War II (1939–1945), Rotary clubs provided emergency relief to

These girls were patients at a hospital in Billings, Montana in 1941. The hospital was run by the local Rotary club.

What specific projects
did Rotarians help
fund during World
War II? What other
organizations did
Rotary clubs partner
with throughout this
conflict? What impact
did their efforts have?
Visit the library or
search online for
the answers to
these questions!

11

people affected by this global conflict. In the years that followed, Rotarians turned their attention to an even wider variety of issues.

Today, Rotary clubs address problems ranging from world hunger to **illiteracy** to **environmental** damage. Local clubs meet weekly to discuss their work. They commit funding and volunteer hours to improving life in both local and international communities. Clubs decide whether to

Many Rotary clubs organize community races to raise money for causes like global hunger.

Are you able to guess
how Rotary clubs pay
for their projects?
(Hint: There are a few
different sources!)
Fund-raisers are
one answer. So are
contributions from
Rotarians and outside
donors. Rotary
clubs also rely on
money from various
investments.

13

support a particular project by asking four questions: Is it the truth? Is it fair to all concerned? Will it build goodwill and better friendships? Will it be beneficial to all?

Rotary clubs depend heavily on the efforts of 1.2 million Rotarians. Members must have a job or be retired. They also have to be committed to serving others. Finally, they must live or work near a Rotary club and attend meetings.

Rotary clubs make sure each of their programs is "beneficial to all." They work with many different cultures and countries.

Think about how the world's 34,000 Rotary clubs are connected. Rotary International—which is headquartered in Evanston, Illinois— helps coordinate these local organizations. It has both volunteers and paid staff with jobs in areas such as accounting, fund-raising, and communication.

POWERFUL PROJECTS

Rotary clubs are made up of business leaders with many different skills and backgrounds. Through teamwork, Rotarians are able to offer unique solutions to community challenges. In some cases, they build wells and sewer systems to ensure that people have access to clean water. In others, they set up health care programs in locations

Rotary clubs around the world build thousands of wells like this one every year.

LOOK!

Go online or visit the library to see photographs of Rotary club programming. What are the volunteers in the pictures doing? How are they creating positive changes within the different communities shown?

where women and children lack medical treatment.

Rotarians are also committed to supporting education. Club **grants** fund literacy classes and introduce the latest technology to poorer areas.

Rotary clubs sponsor youth groups, scholarships, and cultural exchange programs, too. Participants learn leadership skills, the importance of volunteering, and how to promote world peace.

Having access to technology is an important part of a complete education.

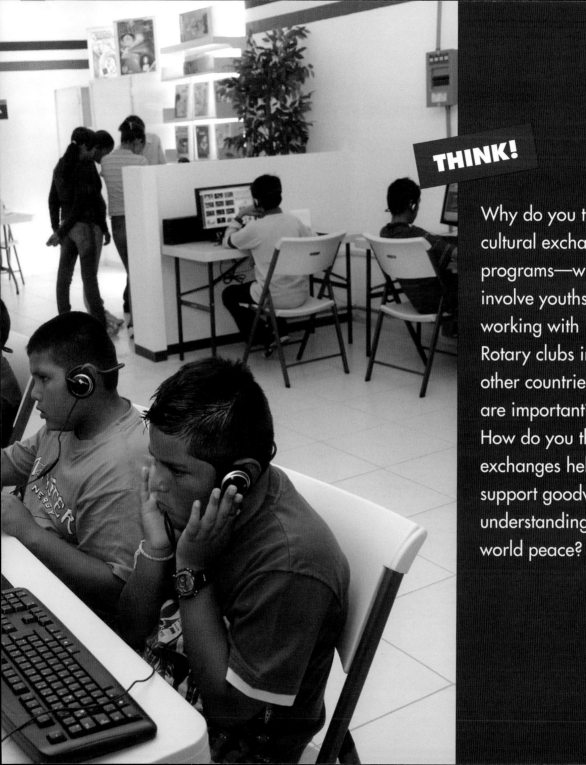

THINK!

Why do you think cultural exchange programs—which involve youths working with Rotary clubs in other countries—are important? How do you think exchanges help support goodwill, understanding, and world peace?

19

Rotarians provide equipment, job training, and other assistance that helps improve economies. They encourage the growth of local businesses and increased opportunities for women and members of minority groups to become leaders in the workplace.

Rotarians have proven their organization is far more than a social group. Rotary clubs are dedicated to serving people and strengthening communities around the world.

Rotarians know that supporting women and minorities helps improve communities all over the world.

After learning more about your local Rotary club, create a mural showing its service projects. First, tape or glue several pieces of poster board together. Then, paint pictures of Rotarians in action! Ask to hang your mural at school.

21

GLOSSARY

donors (DOH-nurz) people who give to charity

economies (ee-KAH-nuh-meez) the processes or systems by which goods and services are produced

environmental (en-vye-ruh-MEN-tuhl) related to the natural surroundings of living things

ethical (EH-thih-kuhl) morally right and good

grants (GRANTZ) sums of money given by an organization

humanitarian (hyoo-man-ih-TER-ee-uhn) relating to people who work to improve the lives of others

illiteracy (ih-LIH-tuh-ruh-see) the state of not knowing how to read or write

immunizations (ih-myu-nuh-ZAY-shuhnz) vaccines that prevent infection by a disease

investments (in-VEST-muhnts) monies spent as part of a financial plan to make a profit

nonprofit (nahn-PRAH-fit) not existing for the main purpose of earning more money than is spent

FIND OUT MORE

BOOKS

Cohn, Jessica. *Improving Communities*. Huntington Beach, CA: Teacher Created Materials, 2013.

Colson, Mary. *Fighting Polio*. New York: Gareth Stevens Publishing, 2015.

Mulder, Michelle. *Every Last Drop: Bringing Clean Water Home*. Victoria, BC: Orca Book Publishers, 2014.

WEB SITES

Neuroscience for Kids—Public-Health Victory: Vaccine-Related Polio Wiped Out in US

faculty.washington.edu/chudler/poliov.html
Review additional information about polio and its effects, as well as its treatment and prevention.

Rotary International—Rotaract, Interact, and RYLA (Rotary Youth Leadership Awards)

www.rotary.org/en/get-involved/join-leaders/rotaract-interact-and-ryla
Read about opportunities for young people to become involved in Rotary club programming.

INDEX

ABOUT THE AUTHOR

Katie Marsico is the
author of more than
200 children's books.
She lives in a suburb
of Chicago, Illinois,
with her husband
and children.

24